Made Up

Framed

two plays with films by Stan's Cafe

ISBN 978-1-913185-09-1

Published by Stan's Cafe
Birmingham, UK
2020

www.stanscafe.co.uk

Made Up © Stan's Cafe 2017
Made Up Photos © Graeme Braidwood 2017
Framed © Stan's Cafe 2002
Framed Photos © Heather Burton 2002
Publication © Stan's Cafe 2020

Contents:

Made Up	4
Bonus Material	
Original production credits	37
Original programme notes	38
The making of *Made Up*	39
Framed	41
Bonus Material	
Credits	48
Early sketch	49
Further ideas on Framed project	51
More Framed thoughts	52

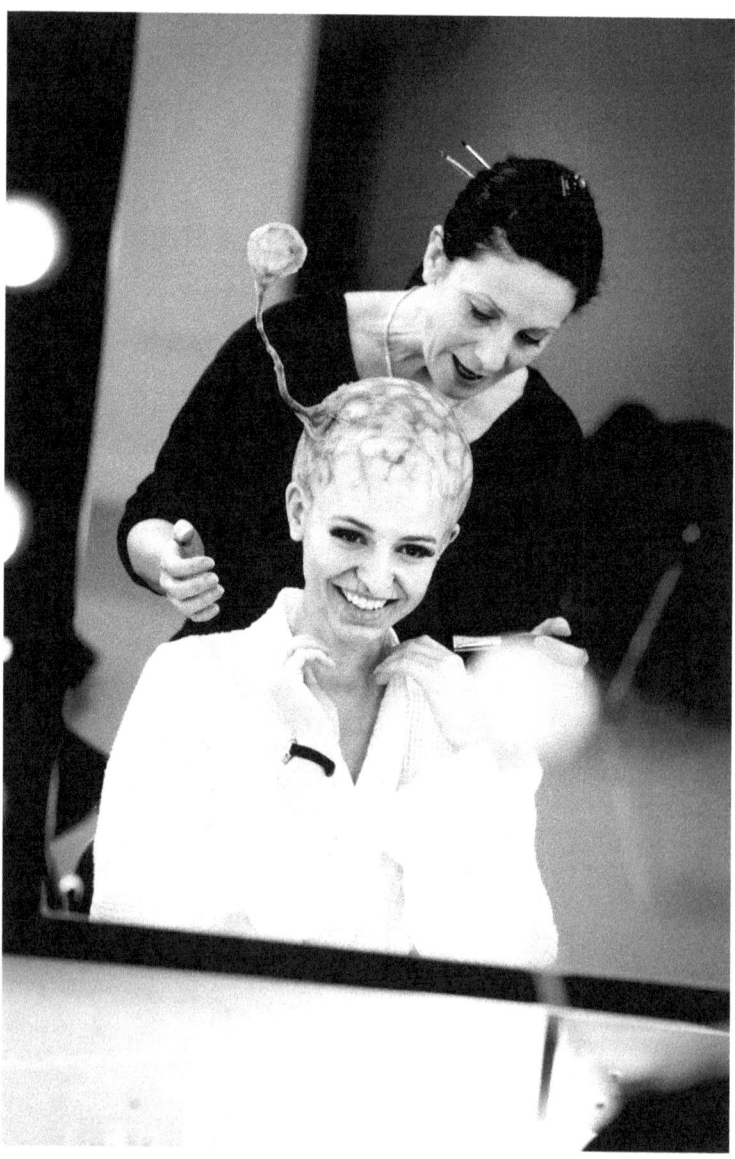

A Note On The Text

Throughout the script is allocated to actors by the initial of their main character. Where this actor plays a different character this is indicated by / and an additional initial.

Within dialogue / indicates that a character is interrupted.

Sue has the radio playing through her working day, this acts as a soundtrack for the play. Occasionally material on the radio station is pertinent to the play's action. The location of these moments but not their content are marked in this script.

For much of the script Sue is applying make up to Kate's face, this process is indicated in stage directions.

A live video relay of Kate's make up being applied is projected on the back wall in diptych either side of that stage. Briefly, when Kate plays her advert role, her role in *The Fire* and in *This Year's Most Beautiful* green screen technology is used to place this live relay over a pre-recorded location. The play concludes with a fragment of footage from Kate's next film, which is a romance set in World War 2. This can be viewed at:

https://vimeo.com/172441653

Some details of lighting cues have been included in the script to give some sense of the play's shifting atmosphere.

Dramatis Personae

Two actors share these roles between them.
Shifts between roles are seamless and the audience
is often left to catch up.

Sue – Make Up Artist

Kate – Young Film Star

Angela – Kate's Agent

Girl Friend

Boy Friend

Mum – Kate's Mother

Alien – Kate in Advertisement Role

Voice Over – Pre-recorded Advertisement

Lexi – Sue's Daughter

Polly – Sue's Sister

Mom – Sue's Mother

Grandmother – Kate in Film Role

Morning

    [LX: 0.5 preset]
    [LX: 1 Houselights out]
    [LX: 2 w/Sue entrance]

S   *[Arrives, takes off coat, turns radio on and starts setting up for the day]*
    [LX: 3 w/Kate Entrance]

K   *[Cue from radio: 'Three Hours'.]* Morning, oh it's so cold isn't it!

S   Morning! I know, I know, don't worry I've got the heater on, it will soon warm up.
    [Gown and clips]

K   Did you have a nice day off?

S   Yes, thank you and you?

K   Yes, fine.

S   Good. Back to the coal-face now.

K   Yes, noses to the grind stone!

S   And I'm all prepped for Scene 54?

K   Yes, there are some rewrites I've got to get my head round but nothing that effects you, obviously. I've got to do a better job than Saturday. I was so rubbish.

S   You looked good from where I was standing, it was the sound department that seemed to be struggling.

K   I think they were just being sweet and covering for me.

S   You're paranoid. Pablo must have got what he wanted or we'd still be there. Anyway, isn't that what editing and dubbing are for?

K   To make up for terrible acting?

S   To emphasis your best bits. Right, ready for the witch hazel?

K   Okay, perform your magic you old witch.
    [Fake witch hazel]

S   Fee fi fo fum.

K   That's for giants. You mean 'hubble bubble toil and trouble'.

S   Oh yes, you're right. 'Hubble bubble' anyway, what's this with the 'old witch' my dear?

K   Sorry, I forgot, 'hands not wands'.

S   Exactly, hands not wands.
    [LX 4: Build around chair]

Previous Work
[Video Relay Up]
[Warm base applied]

S   You know you look really familiar, it's been bugging me the whole shoot. I've seen you somewhere before *The Fire*. I want to say that it was at my mum's house, but that's ridiculous isn't it? You didn't know my mum did you?
K   *[Laughing]* No.
S   No it wasn't there, but it was like it was there.
K   How strange.
    Some people just have those familiar faces don't they.
S   Some.
K   I'm terrible at putting names to faces, I wish I was better, it would be so useful. What I need is to take a Polaroid of everyone I get introduced to and write their name in the white bit at the bottom. Then I've got a revision aid. Can I get away with that, as my quirky thing, an art project? That's it I just say it's an art project. What do you think?
S   Are you sure you weren't in anything before *The Fire*?
K   No, no, no films no.
S   No films, but something else, that wasn't a film?
K   No.
S   Something that was on TV?
K   No.
S   Kate you are lying to me, I can tell, make up artists can always tell.
K   It wasn't anything. I don't count it.
S   It was something, it was on the TV at my Mum's, one of the lifestyle channels she… oh my God! You were…
    [Screams, imitating the advert]
S   I loved that advert.
K   It was the worst thing ever! You mustn't tell anyone. Really, it's so embarrassing!
S   Everyone has to start somewhere *[screams again]*.
K   Shut up!
S   Hold still. I've seen you at six in the morning, with no sleep and a hangover, I don't believe you've ever woken 'in an Alien's skin', not in your whole life, but then who has? What does it actually mean? 'Waking in an Alien's skin'?
K   I don't know!
S   I suppose if you'd been swallowed in the night by an alien, like a huge python, then you'd have woken in an Alien's skin.

K   I don't think moisturiser would help you much in that situation.
S   No, even I couldn't save you then. 'Hands not wands darling'! Who comes up with that crap?
K   I don't know, I didn't write it, I just said it... quite badly.
S   Does anyone ever recognise you from that?
K   No, not really. I think your mum may be the only person to ever watch that network.

What's Wrong?
   [Highlight under eyes]
K   I think I'm going to ask them if I can do some of the stunts. I fancy the window ledge action.
S   They'll green screen that surely.
K   No, remember Pablo likes to keep it as real as he can. They're planning to get a stunt team in but it's only a window ledge for heaven's sake and I'm supposed to look scared, so there's no trouble there.
   [Pause]
K   Did I tell you I've started yoga? I'm following this guru woman

	on-line. She's really good.
S	You'd be better off finding a real person to work with you.
K	She is real.
S	No, someone in the room with you, who can check you're doing it right, yoga's all about the detail. Don't blink.
K	She explains it really well, and uses a skeleton and there are close ups and diagrams and everything.
S	*[Doubtful]* It sounds brilliant.
K	It really is, she's totally charismatic, she reminds me of you.
S	Ha! *[stops applying make up]*
K	It's true. She's got this aura about her and she's so lithe, like a whip, or a whippet or something. What's wrong?
S	Nothing, you remind me of someone, that's all. *[resumes make up]*
K	Someone you miss?
S	Yes, sort of.
K	Your daughter?
S	Lexi? No.
K	A friend?
S	No.
K	I'm sorry.
S	It's not your fault dear.
K	Do I look like them?
S	No, no, not at all, it's just that energy, that enthusiasm, that joy for life. You remind me of me when I was younger.
K	Why does that make you sad?
S	It doesn't. It makes me happy. *[Powder face]* *[Start eyeshadow]*

Kate's Mum

S	Oh yes, how was it with your mum?
K	Predictable.
S	That bad!
K	Good at first, nice, nice to see her, but then… she doesn't understand, she says she does but…
S	No one understands what it's like.
K	I'm not sure she even tries really.
S	Has she come on set before?
K	She came out for *The Fire* – but she only really came hoping to meet Nigel.

S   Oh dear!
K   No, it was fine, he was charming; you know what he's like with 'the older woman'. She was charmed.
S   He can certainly turn it on, when he can be bothered. He never bothers with me. He doesn't see me.
K   And that bothers you? *[Opens eyes]*
S   Ha! No, his letching makes my skin crawl.
K   Mine too!
S   That 'silver fox' thing he does is almost as bad.
K   "Absolutely charmed my dear".
S   I'm happy to be off his radar.
       You didn't have much to do with him in that did you?
K   No, just a couple of scenes with him safely behind a desk.
       Sue, you're not invisible are you?
S   Mostly. Close your eyes.
K   Do you mind?
S   Sometimes, sometimes.
       [LX 5: Check down Cover]
       [Lips]
       [RADIO MOMENT]
       [Eyebrows]
       [LX 6: Restore]

Vlogger

K   Have you heard of the K Formula?
S   No, who's it by?
K   Enchanta.
S   Eugh, no thank you!
K   I thought you might say that. My sister's latest post is about it.
S   What does it do?
K   It's a cream you apply to your face just before you go to bed, it sets through the night and then you peel it off in the morning. It's supposed to rehydrate and exfoliate simultaneously. It's supposed to be anti-ageing. I think the K is for Keratin.
S   Sounds horrific. What did she think?
K   She liked it. She's filmed herself putting it on and getting into bed, then she's put in a time passing effect and filmed herself getting up and taking it off in the morning. The commentary's good and she's getting much better at the editing.
S   How old is she?
       [Blusher]
K   Seventeen.

S   Ah, I see how an anti-aging cream is an essential product for her. How old did she look when she woke up, twelve?
K   No, still seventeen but once she'd put her make up on she was up to about twenty four.
S   Useful for the nightclubs.
K   Oh she doesn't go out, she spends all her time vlogging and revising for her A-levels.
S   She sounds like the model daughter.
K   Ah she'd love to be the 'model' daughter but she's waiting to have her brace taken out, then she's going to get a portfolio together.
S   A brace could work, geek-chic.
K   No, she thinks it's more 'ugly' than 'arresting'.
S   Is she okay?
K   What do you mean?
S   She's okay with herself, in herself, eating?
K   Oh yes I don't worry about that, she and her friends are all about loving themselves and each other just the way they are, 'go girl'. The make up's all just a hobby really.
S   That's nice.
K   You should have a vlog.
S   Ha!
K   *Sue Harman's Big Screen Make Up Tips*. Today, how to look like you've been crying all night.
S   Oh that'll be a hit!
    Here [hands K a few bottles]
    [Mascara]
K   What are these?
S   Samples, we get loads of them, I never use them but I thought your sister might like to move on from the K Formula.
K   Wow, that's so kind. She'll love this; she can't get enough of the freebies.
S   I bet she's enjoying having a famous big sister.
K   Yes, Angela's worried she's enjoying it a bit too much. She's changed her name on the blog to Beccs Sky.
S   Oh.
K   I don't mind. It's not doing any harm.
S   Except it's all reflecting back on you, whatever she does. She's going to have to be careful.
K   I like it, it's cute. She's my sister, I'm not ashamed of her.
S   I know you're not but she is cashing in on you and like it or not that does reflect back on you.

K I know, I know! That's what Angela said. She said it makes me look cheap. She wants me to tell Becca to change her name back.
S That's going to be a tough conversation.
K Yeah, I don't want to do it, but if I don't then Angela will get Phoebe to do it and that will be worse.
S What about your mum?
K She'd not understand. She'd be on Becca's side, I'm on Becca's side… God I hate this!
[LX 7: Focus down on chair]
[Video feed off]
[Poised Moment Of Glamour look]
[LX 8: Restore]

Lexi Hairbrush

[Brush 'hair']
K/L Owch!
S Hold still, it's knotted.
K/L Owww!
S I don't know what you've got in this.
K/L Nothing!
S It's sticky, it's jam or toffee or eugh!
K/L I'll do it myself.
S You won't young lady, I can't trust you to do it properly.
K/L I can do my own hair you know!
S You had lots of chances and I'm not letting you go to school like this.
[Wig off]
K/L Dad does.
S Well he shouldn't, I'll speak to him about that later.
K/L Nan does.
S I'm sure she doesn't.
K/L No one at school cares anyway.
S I'm sure they do.
[LX 9]
[Video back on]

Sue's Lexi Story

[Pale base (inc lips)]
K How old's Lexi?
S Twenty two. No, twelfth of August, twenty three!
K What does she do?

S   I… I don't really see her any more.
K   Oh, I'm sorry, how come?
S   Well, we fell out a few years ago. This job isn't very family friendly.
K   It sounds tough.
S   Lexi's dad was freelance as well. We tried to juggle it between us but there were tensions.
K   What does he do?
S   He's a designer - theatre and film sets.
    It was easy at first because neither of us got much work. We had a great time but then it started to take off for me a bit, then the *Titan Trilogy* came along and we discussed it and it was too good to turn down but it meant I was away so much.
K   That's tough.
    [Powder]
S   Yeah and then in the middle of that Tony got a big job offer and I couldn't ask him not to do it, but he made that decision anyway. He found smaller bitty stuff closer to home and we muddled through with my mum and friends and me doing insane late-night driving and he became resentful and I was knackered and fractious and poor Lexi, I think she picked up on all that, she became so difficult and that made things worse. I was so furious and tired all the time.
    [White Eyes]
K   How old was she when you split up?
S   Fourteen.
K   Oh it's difficult.
S   We tried to keep it civilised, but it ended up pretty ugly and I think Lexi lost respect for us both. She moved to London as soon as she could and like I said, I don't really see her any more.
K   Do you see Tony?
S   We used to see each other around occasionally, unexpectedly, it was always pretty painful. Then one day he was with a young woman. He introduced me to her: Lucy. The next thing I heard they were in New York together.
K   He emigrated!
S   Off Broadway. She was American. She seemed nice, young but nice.
K   Was Lexi already in London by this point?
S   No, this was about a year after the split, a year before she went. He was always more selfish than he'd admit.

K   Oh Sue, I'm sorry.
    [Circles on cheeks]
S   Don't be. I was a crap mother, a crap wife, for a while I think I was even a crap make up artist.
K   I'm sure you weren't. You can't do everything.
S   Oh, I think I failed at most things. The evidence is pretty clear.

Terry #1

[Brush and pencil brows]
S   Tell me about Terry.
K   There's nothing to tell.
S   Is he coming out?
K   What do you mean?
S   Is he coming out on location?
K   Oh, no, he's busy. He's shooting a documentary in China.
S   How long have you been seeing each other?
K   A year or so.
S   And you like him?
K   Of course, he's lovely, very easy going, very considerate.
S   He does sound lovely. He looks a dish. Do you think he's 'a keeper'?
K   Why all the questions? Let's leave it shall we?
S   I'm sorry. You're right.
    [LX 10: Down]
    [RADIO MOMENT]
    [Lips]
    [LX 11: Restore]

Spotted

S   *[Apply spot]* No sign of Boris returning this morning?
K   No, I'm pleased to be shot of that little git.
S   I bet. Terry must have been getting jealous. "He comes unbidden in the night".
    Don't worry, he would be no match for Touché Éclat.
K   I'd only popped out for a pint of bloody milk, you'd think that would be okay wouldn't you!
S   But you were 'spotted' and Boris got his own close up.
K   Should have got his own agent!
S   A chat show! 'Boris takes the Pus'?
K   Enough with the puns.
S   Sorry, an on the spot fine?
K   I said enough!

S   We could listen to him on Spotify.
K   Can I remind you that our relationship is based on a firm foundation.
S   Ah, you can conceal nothing from me.
K   Ha!
S   He got his own Facebook group didn't he?
K   Boris? No, it was a Twitter account, a bunch of hilarious undergrads somewhere.
[Pause] At least it kept them off trolling for an hour or two.
S   You'll be more careful in the future.
K   I don't see why I should.
S   Never go out without foundation and lippy.
K   Sod that, I was going round the corner for a pint of milk, it wasn't a performance.
S   That's what you thought, but clearly you had an audience. From now on you'd better assume you will always have an audience.
K   What do you mean 'from now on'!
S   Okay, before you were a young woman going for a pint of milk, you got attention but not expectation, now you're Kate Sky going for a pint of milk and you're 'on' in a completely different way; but you know that.
K   Yes, I'm 'on' pretty much everywhere.
S   Not in here.
[Get wig]
K   No, no, not in here.
Phoebe thought it was great news.
S   What?
[Wig on]
K   She phoned me up; she said "Great news – you're in Heat". She said "If they care that much about your spot you've made it". My mum was the same, proud that I shared a page with Kim K's camel toe, Beyonce's VPL and J Law's armpit stubble. It's madness.
S   I know. Always remember that, always remember it's madness.
[Video relay off. Green-screen on]
[LX 12: Video mode]

The Fire
K   "Lord Thomas, I have never been so offended in my life, what a woman's true complexion is, is of no one's business but their own".

Next Role
[Emily handed wipes and wig off]
[LX 13: Return]
S/A   What do you think of the Gold Vision script? Brilliant isn't it!
K   Yeah amazing.
S/A   And it looks like Eric's going to sign so I think that's yours and it looks like it is going to be opposite Tom, so that pushes it onto another level and we can push for a good bit more.
K   That's great.
S/A   And it will fit your schedule perfectly. It's mostly being filmed in Elstree so at a push you could do it from home and for that first section they're looking at the Seychelles.
K   Yeah, I know. Angela, I don't know if it's right for me.
S/A   Why?
K   Well the… the whole 'wild woman' thing.
S/A   It's a challenging part, it'll stretch your range, it'll open more roles up for you, it's what you've always wanted and The Academy love all that big make up, transformational, learning to speak acting. I really think this could be big for you Kit.

K	I don't want to be naked.
S/A	Kit love, we've talked about this.
K	I don't like the idea.
S/A	It's integral to the story and it's Eric, you can trust Eric, he's going to be tasteful. *[Patch up pale base]* *[LX 13.5: closer]* *[Video Relay Back]*
K/Gf	I don't, it's not, I, I'm not ready.
S/Bf	You would if you loved me. I'll send you a photo.
K/Gf	I don't want of photo of you, not like that.
S/Bf	Don't you love me?
K/Gf	I do, I just don't want a/
S/Bf	I miss you.
K/Gf	I miss you too.
S/Bf	So send me a photo.
K/Gf	No.
S/Bf	Why not?
K/Gf	You'll show it to your friends.
S/Bf	I'd never do that. *[LX 14: Restore]* *[Sink temples and cheeks]*
S/A	We'll put a clause in the contract specifying what they can and can't show. It'll be a closed set/
K	I don't feel comfortable with the idea.
S/A	Kit, there will always be love scenes, it's part of life.
K	My private life, it's my body I need to/
S/A	Let's talk about it when I see you, it's an amazing opportunity.
K	I don't want to be looked at in that way.
S/A	In what way do you think people are going to be looking at you? What people are you worried about?
K	I don't know! My family, my friends, my neighbours, people in the street, strangers, teenage boys, sad old men!
S/A	Kate what kind of film do you think this is going to be? They're aiming for Certificate 15. It will be perfectly innocent and imagining it to be anything else means you're censoring your own career and I can't let you do that. Let's talk about it when I see you. It's an amazing opportunity.

On-Line Dating

[LX 15: Centre main]
[Age nostrils, bags, acne, chin mouth]

K	So, did you register?
S	Yes.
K	Oh well done you, did you go 'bright and bubbly' or 'intelligent and energetic'?
S	'Smart and sassy'.
K	Brilliant.
S	'Bright and bubbly' made me sound Page 3, 'intelligent and energetic' is like I want to go hiking around archaeological digs. With 'smart and sassy' - you're going to have fun!
K	True. Which photo did you go for?
S	The windswept one.
K	That's good. You're sure that's not 'archaeological dig'?
S	I think it is but as I'm already 'smart and sassy' I can afford to look a bit 'outdoorsy' and I like my smile in that one.
K	You can change your profile once it's up can't you.
S	Why? Don't you like 'smart and sassy and windswept'?
K	No, no, I do, I'm just wondering, if it's… you.
S	It's definitely me, I recognise myself.
	[Restart]
K	No I mean…
S	It's so difficult with the photo. If you go too glam you get all the sleazy guys. If you don't go glam enough no one's interested.
K	Oh.
S	You don't like it do you? You think I should use the one with the cleavage.
K	The ball gown? No, I like the Christmas one, you look stunning.
S	That is a nice one but I don't think it looks like me, do you? I don't want them to be disappointed when they finally see me.
K	You're crazy? Are you listening to yourself? Are you looking at yourself?
S	I don't know, maybe I should change it to the ball gown.
K	Why don't you just not have a picture?
S	Now you're the one who's being crazy.
K	No, then they'd have to judge you by who you are not what you look like.
S	What you look like is part of who you are. Trust me, it's my job, I know these things. Anyway, if you don't post a picture people will assume you were a monster.
K	I suppose.
S	I know.

Kate's Mum Phone

[LX 16: Glitch and change return]
[Wax eyebrows]

K Mum, I've told you lots of times.
S/Mu Well I don't remember. But you're enjoying it? *[Look]*
K Yes, they're all very nice people, but it's really difficult.
S/Mu Good. I'm still worried about that fence.
K Oh dear, it's still not fixed?
S/Mu No. I asked Ray, but you see he's been doing a lot of work for Jan and he's promised to sort out Meryl's leaky bay before he can get round to look at it. *[look]*
K Well can, can you not ask Trevor to nail something across it until it's fixed properly? Just to stop you worrying.
S/Mu Well I don't like to ask him at this time of year because it/
K Mum, he won't mind it'll just take him a moment.
S/Mu But he's awfully busy.
K Listen, mum he won't mind.
S/Mu No, I don't want to bother him.
K Then you're going to have to live with a broken fence for a bit aren't you.
S/Mu But it does worry me, people can look in, it's not safe.
K Listen Mum, do you want me to get it sorted out?
S/Mu Well how are you going to do that? From where you are?
K I, I don't know, I'll make some calls, I'll check it out on-line, there's got to be a fencing firm that will be able to do it.
S/Mu Well I don't want just anyone coming round, you never know who people are!
K Listen Mum, I've really go to go!
S/Mu Oh, why? *[Look]*
[Powder]
K Because I'm on set.
S/Mu If you must.
K Did you get the flowers?
S/Mu Oh yes.
K Are they nice?
S/Mu Mmm.
K They were supposed to come in a vase, did they?
S/Mu Yes, I think they did.
K Okay, so long as you got them on time.
S/Mu Yes, they came on Tuesday when Jan was here, she was very impressed.
K Good okay, I've got to go *[hangs up]* Aaaaah!

[LX 16.3: Back in Winnebago]
You know, honestly, sometimes...
It's like having a kid, I imagine.
S   Lexi was never that bothered about fences.
K   Touché.
S   Oh I didn't mean it like that. You're right, high maintenance... But you'll miss her when she's not around to piss you off.
K   Are we talking your mum or my mum now? Or Lexi?
S   All of them I suppose.
K   Sorry, can I just have a moment.
[LX 16.5: Something]
[Poised moment of ill look]
[LX 17: Central Main]
[Blot and highlight brows]

Kate Crisis of Confidence

K   Sue, will you always be with me?
S   If I'm free, I'll come whenever you need me, wherever you are my dear.
K   I think I'll always need you.
S   You won't, there's plenty can do what I do.
K   No. Promise you'll always come.
S   I can't promise that my dear, you know I can't. If I'm free, I'll come.
K   I'll get Angela to make it part of the contract 'no you, no me', simple.
S   So you're 'A' list now are you? Spielberg will hold the whole production till Muggins here has finished on Coronation Street.
K   I don't do Spielberg and you don't do Corrie.
S   No, not yet, but I think it'd be nice to be settled. I'm knackered.
K   You're not you're brilliant; you're the most vital person I know.
S   I'm a good make up artist my dear. If I looked as knackered as I feel that'd be embarrassing. I can do 'awake' in my sleep. I did this *[her own face]* in my sleep this morning.
K   What time were you up?
S   Four.
K   That's brutal!
[LX 17.5: Glitch]
S   She didn't mean it.
K   Even so.
S   She was hurt and I can see why, who wouldn't react like that?

K   Not everyone.
S   She was scared so she lashed out.
K   And you were hurt so you responded.
S   But I'm her mum, I was the grown up. I should have absorbed it and not shouted back. Shouting back never helps.
K   Maybe.
S   I should have seen it coming earlier; I can't believe I didn't.
K   What would you have done?
S   Something.
K   I'm sorry.
[LX 18: Close in more]
S   It's not your fault my dear. Nothing's your fault. You've got to stop thinking like that. Don't absorb it, let it bounce off. You've got to develop that shell madam, toughen up honey.
K   That's not me; I'm not tough.
S   You wouldn't be here if you weren't tough.
[Video relay off when make up is finished]
K   I'm pretty, I fluked the graduation show and Eric is a genius and Angela's unbelievable, it's happening *to* me, I'm here because.. I don't know, because of Eric and Angela and now Pablo, who knows Eric so there's that and I don't know what I'm doing. I stand where I'm told, I don't even know how to say these lines. I hate my voice, I'm not tough, I'm… they're going to find out!
S   You think you're the only pretty girl there is?
K   No.
S   No, of course you're not. Do you think there are prettier girls than you?
K   Yes.
S   Well I don't know, who's to say? But I know one thing, 'pretty' may get you in the door but after that it's talent my dear, talent and guts and confidence and all your other qualities. It's you who's got you here, not Eric, not Angela, not 'pretty'. You're plenty tough enough my girl.
You just have to put on a brave face.
[Alien cowl on]
[LX 19: Video moment, green screen]

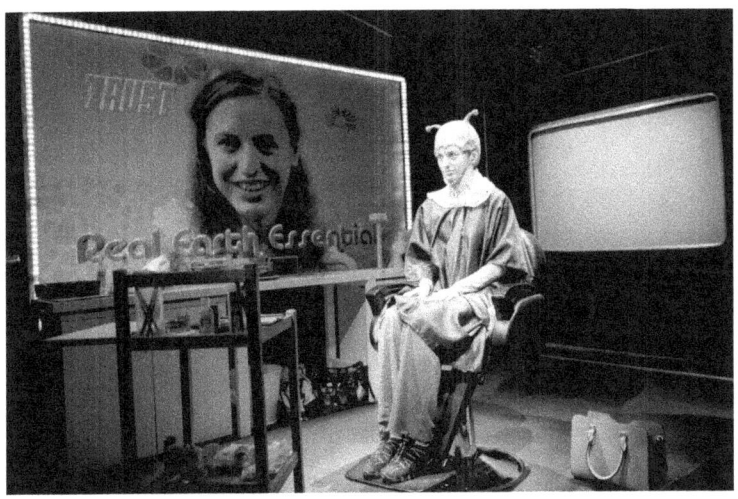

Real Earth Essentials
K/Al *[Tentatively touches face, turns to camera and screams]* "When you wake in an Alien's skin"...
V/O ...trust Real Earth Essentials to restore the real you.
    [LX 20: Return]

Lexi Argument.
    [Remove cowl and freshen base with pale ivory]
K/L It's just a name, I don't see why he's so angry.
S   It's his name and he doesn't want you changing it. He's proud of you and /
K/L Pshh, proud! Whatever. He's an arrogant knob.
S   Lex that's enough!
K/L You said it yourself.
S   That's different.
K/L I don't see how.
S   He was my husband, I can call him what I want. You can't.
K/L He's my dad and he's an arrogant knob and I don't want his name.
S   If you call yourself Harman it'll make things even worse than they are now Lex.
K/L I'm not gonna be Harman.
S   Right, so what name are you going to have?
K/L Nothing, just Lexi.

S   Just Lexi?
K/L Yeah.
S   Like Kylie… Madonna!
K/L Don't laugh at me!
S   I'm not.
K/L You never take me seriously, you treat me like a kid, you both do.
S   We both take you very seriously, that's partly why we row so much.
K/L Wot so it's my fault now?
S   What? No! Lexi. Don't be ridiculous. I didn't mean/
K/L There you go AGAIN.
S   What!
K/L You're not taking me seriously!
S   When!
K/L Just then, you said I'm ridiculous.
S   I didn't say you *are* ridiculous, I said. Oh I give up! Close your eyes.
    [Video relay up]
    [Powder and eyeshadow]
    [LX 20.5]

Female Tarzan

K   *[Hold's hand up]*
S/A *[Leaves her]*
K   Hi Angela.
S/A Kit, Pheebs says you're still worried about the Gold Vision Script.
K   Yeah, it doesn't feel right for me yet.
S/A It's not coming round again honey, take it or leave it and you need to take it.
K   There are plenty of other options.
S/A Not like this, this is special Kit, Eric's very excited about you being on board.
K   Angela I'm not 'on board'. I'm looking at other things.
S/A Kit, this is not the time to step back. We need you out there, very visible, in a great vehicle, with lots of exposure, then you can do anything you want, you can pick and choose. Then if you want to do an independent you'll be in a position to raise the money, you can be on board as a producer. If you don't push yourself forward aggressively now, none of that is possible. The Gold Vision script is the only thing I can allow

you to do now Kit love.
[White eye shadow]

K   I don't want to do it Angela.

S/A   You're not thinking about this clearly. Let me get Eric to talk to you about how he'd handle those early scenes, it really won't be what you think, he can explain what's possible.

K   Angela, it's not just that, it's… I think… I think it's naff.

S/A   It's Sydney Wiseman, it's Butch Greenman, it's Tony Amichi, Gold Vision's 'A' Team Kit, it is not naff!

K   It's *Pygmalion*, it's *My Fair Lady*, it's *Pretty Woman*,

S/A   All great films. It's original, it's inspirational, it's arresting, it's empowering, it's a female Tarzan.

K   There you are, a female Tarzan!

S/A   Listen Kit, we're boarding, I've got to go love but Gold Vision need an answer by the end of week, I'm going to get Eric to call you and Pheebs will speak to you tomorrow about how we're shaping up the terms.

K   Angela! Aaaarh!
[LX 21]
[RADIO MOMENT]
[Lips. White eye shadow]

Sue & Dad

[Eyeliner and eyebrows]
[LX 22]

K/P   Michael should be putting a shift in. He's only forty minutes away, most of the time he's closer than you.

S   Polly, I know, but you know he's useless. He'd just be feeding Dad take-outs.

K/P   It's learnt helplessness Sue and you know it.

S   I know.

K/P   Mum taught us all the same. He's got no excuses.

S   Yes, I know.

K/P   He can run a firm but the sight of a raw pork chop baffles him? I don't think so.

S   No.

K/P   What use has he actually been over the last few weeks Sue? What's he actually done?

S   You're right.

K/P   He's stepped in like a hero to deal with the probate, he read the eulogy and assumed the role of toastmaster at the wake, but what has he actually done? Where was he when it came to

	going through her cupboards and emptying her wardrobe?
S	Listen Polly, I'm sorry I haven't been more help, this has came at a really bad time, if you had left it I would have been able to do it in a few weeks.
K/P	Sue, you did loads and you've been brilliant with Dad, I don't know how you have the patience. It's made sense for me to do it while I'm over here. I'm sorry I can't stay longer. You shouldn't have to deal with all this on your own. That's what I mean about Michael.
S	He's not so bad. He's promised to help find a place for Dad.
K/P	Right and you know the home could be nearer him than you. It makes more sense that way.
S	Yes, we have discussed that.
K/P	Well don't let it slip.
S	No. And Michael's going to have to help out for the next few weeks because I'm on location.
K/P	Oh that's great, a good start. Is it anything exciting?
S	*This Year's Most Beautiful*.
K/P	Most beautiful what?
S	That's the name of the film – *This Year's Most Beautiful*.
K/P	Oh, okay. Who would I know in it?
S	It's directed by Pablo Mendoza, it's staring Dev MacIntosh, Kate Sky, Jonathan Cruikshank/
K/P	Oh she's fabulous! I'm so jealous of her. She always looks so amazing. Has she genuinely got fabulous skin or is that just the magic of cinema? Please tell me it's all a cosmetic illusion.
S	That's a trade secret, you know me, I cannot divulge.
K/P	Sue don't be so such a/
S	I'm joking, of course she's got great skin but you've got great skin too.
K/P	I have?
S	Of course you have, you always have had.
K/P	It makes up for the wonky nose and big ears.
S	Big heart and wonky sense of humour more like. Taxi's here.
K/P	Oh no, I've got to go.
S	Yeah. Text me from the airport.
K/P	I will. Don't let Michael let you do it all.
S	No, I won't I promise.
K/P	I'm going to hound him from across the Atlantic.
S	Thank you. Skype me when you're home.
K/P	I will do.
S	Love to Stuart and the boys.

K/P Of course, give Dad a hug - tell him from me.
S   I will.
     [Nose piece & wig]
     [LX 23]

Paparazzi
     [LX 24]
S/N Kate, Kate, Kate give us a smile!
K/N Terry this way, Terry, Terry. Is it true you're splitting up?
S/N Give us a smile Kate.
K/N Kate are you pregnant?
S/N Kate are you having an affair with Seth Lions?
K/N Smile Kate.
S/N Terry are you coming out?

Scarring and Tattoo
     [LX 25]
     [K's right sleeve is rolled up revealing scars from self harm cuts]
S   Look away and shield your face. Don't breathe in.
K/L I'm a million miles away, upstairs, at Dad's house, in Nan's spare room.
     "Where am I tomorrow? Who is picking me up?"
     I'm in detention, at the bus stop, in the shopping centre.
     It's the underpass, the park, I'm on my own.
     [Tattoo revealed]
     I am out of control and now, for these moments, I have control.

[Get alcohol, brush/cotton wool and towel]
"Are you in tonight?"
"I'm at Nathan's". Ask me please. Help me.
"Leave me alone. It's none of your business".
I am out of control and now, for these moments, I have control.
[Start applying alcohol]
"You're too late". "I'm not bothered".
"Don't worry mum, it's all healed over".

S   We can remove this using alcohol. It won't take long and it shouldn't hurt. I'm just going to drench the whole area with alcohol until it all becomes loose.
There we are, that's better. We can lift it all away now.
It should all come off in one piece.
[Scarring is off, start applying the tattoo]

S   I see you in London, a shared house, in… Deptford. New Cross. You are at college, a foundation course. You work in a restaurant.

K/L   Maybe.

S   You don't know your grandma's dead. You're on the pill.

K/L   Maybe.

S   You're building your life without me. You're smiling again. Your life is full of mystery. Are you sure you want me to do this?
[Ready for tattoo reveal]

K/L   Yes please. I seek comfort where I can find it.

S   Your rage has become your passion and your stubbornness your strength.
[Drying tattoo with towel]
It's permanent… but we can always cover it up.
[RADIO MOMENT]
[LX 26: Return]

Other Future Roles

[Base lines wrinkles nose 'w's crows feet]

S   So what do you do next?

K   Go on holiday, remind myself what my flat looks like, see if my cat remembers me.

S   No, I meant after that, work.

K   Well that's what the row's about really.
There's all sorts out there, there's loads of stuff like *The Fire* but I don't want to do that again. Then there's talk of a sequel to this

S   What, that's an actual thing? I thought that was just on-set

K   gossip.
K   No it's a thing, but it would be way down the line. There's more stuff like this, even though we've not finished it yet.
S   And there's more Alien Skin stuff?
K   No! Of course there are always adverts but we're steering clear of those for now.
S   There's the Female Tarzan thing.
K   I'm being mean, I'm sure it will be great but…
S   You don't want to be the wild thing tamed?
K   Angela's so keen, it's difficult.
S   Does she show you everything that comes in?
K   Everything credible. There'd be too much otherwise.
S   You're a lucky girl to have choices.
K   I know, I know, but… most of them don't feel like choices. They're multiple versions of the same thing; it's a choice but… I don't know. This is working isn't it, why would I want to stop doing the thing that's working?
S   Why would you?
K   I don't know, I think I'm crazy. Why wouldn't I be satisfied with all this?
S   Because…
K   Because somehow it's too easy, suspiciously easy, does that make sense?
S   Not really.

[LX 27]

K/L   It's like everyone expects me to play this role and they're lovely to me when I'm in that role but that role's not me, but then it must be me because everyone tells me how natural I am in it and sometimes it is natural and it's easy, but because they make it easy and it's all set up to be easy, but… I can see that if I do this again, just one more time, that's it, that's the only way people will think of me and I can do more than that, more than this.
S   Of course you can. You can do whatever you want.
K/L   But I can't, can I?
S   What's stopping you?
K/L   People think I'm weird because of what I look like.
S   It's your choice, why make yourself look like this?
K/L   Because I like it.
S   So do I.
K/L   You don't
S   I do, it's your personal style, a bit Siouxsie Sioux, a bit Marilyn

	Manson, a bit Emo/
K/L	It's not Emo, stop talking about things you know nothing about.
S	Well, I'm sorry for not being shocked by your rebellion.
K/L	I'm not rebelling; I'm just being me.
S	So what do you want to do?
K/L	Hair & beauty.
S	That's it?
K/L	What?
S	That's your ambition?
K/L	What's wrong with Hair and Beauty?
S	Nothing.
K/L	You do Hair and Beauty.
S	*[Deep breath]* There's nothing wrong with Hair and Beauty but don't just do it because your mates are.
K/L	I'm not, I like make up.
S	Cosmetic or theatrical or medical or forensic or face painting at festivals? You see, if you don't know what you want to do you need to keep your options open and that's by doing 'A' levels.
K/L	Ugh!
S	Do your 'A' levels and then see how you feel, if you still want to do Hair and Beauty, do Hair and Beauty.
K/L	'A' levels will be so boring and sixth form is totally lame.
S	You can do art. You like art, you're talented, you would enjoy that and you could do English and, and why not try something new?
K/L	Like what?
S	Well, Sociology.
K/L	What's that?
S	It's about society, why the world's like it is, how things work as they do. Why everything's "so unfair". It involves lots of arguing; you'd enjoy it.
K/L	Mum!
S	I'm sorry, but I am being serious, you should look into it, you'd love it.
K/L	Did you do it?
S	Not at 'A' level, at college.
K/L	You did art.
S	I did, with a bit of sociology thrown in. Now that's a place you'd love. Central St. Martins. *[LX 28: Shift]*

Advice

S It's in London

K/Mo Why would you want to go there?

S It's the best place for fashion in the country Mum, it's where everything's happening. Mave Jones, remember, from the year above me, she went there last year; she says it's fantastic. Mr. Evans said my portfolio is good enough and that if I can get an interview then they're bound to take me, he's writing me a reference.

K/Mo Sue Where would you live? Have you thought this through?

S I don't know, I'll find digs, the college has lists. I'll travel in on the tube, or a bus, I might even get a bicycle – that would be cheap.

K/Mo I don't want you in one of those squats.

S Oh I think it would be brilliant. If a building's been left empty by its rich owner why shouldn't poor people move in?

K/Mo I don't want you living with those people.

S 'Those people' might be nice people Mum. What do you mean 'those people'?

K/Mo You know, anarchists, 'Ban the Bombers', drop outs. Your dad will have a fit.

S He won't notice, and you don't need to worry Mum, I can look after myself now. I'm a big girl!

K/Mo Sue there's more to the world than you know.

S And that's why I'm going to London.
[LX 28.5 (copy of 27)]

K/Mo It'll upset your mum.

S/L She'll be pleased, I'll be out of her hair.

K/Mo That's not true Alexis.

S/L Lexi.

K/Mo I'm sorry – Lexi.

S/L We argue all the time about everything.

K/Mo Why do you think that is? Is it because she doesn't care? Well?

S/L She's always having a go.

K/Mo You haven't answered my question.

S/L What's that?

K/Mo Would she argue with you if she didn't care about you?

S/L No.

K/Mo So how do we sort this out?
[LX 29: Return to main]

S I don't know, somehow I've got to get in contact with her again.

K   I can't believe it's not possible to track someone down these days.
S   I know but believe me I've tried everything I can think of, friends, social media, colleges, all sorts.
K   What about her bank account?
S   It's data protection, they won't tell me anything.
K   The police?
S   Not interested.
K   Really?
S   She's not technically a missing person.
K   We just need to put some adverts out, from you to her, in magazines she might read, or a big billboard somewhere, in South London. Somewhere that will get loads of publicity.
S   Mmm.
K   Sue, I could put an appeal out or something, in an interview… or is that a bit weird? Oh I'm sorry, that is a bit, that's stupid. I'm sorry.
S   It's sweet my dear.
K   Forget I said all that.
S   It's okay.
[LX 30]
[RADIO MOMENT]
[LX 31: Main]

WW2 Script
S   Do people send scripts directly to you?
K   All the time. It drives Angela crazy.
S   Because she's the agent?
K   Of course, I can see her point, but it's sweet and it's flattering.
S   See if you're still saying that in ten years.
K   If I'm still doing this in ten years. If people are still casting me in ten years.
S   What will you be then 32? 33? You never know, you may have made the transition to 'character actor' by then
K   Oi *[tries to thump her]* I play characters now thank you.
S   I know, I'm teasing my dear. I bet Angela hates you getting scripts direct because you actually read them don't you?
K   Some.
S   What are the latest?
K   One set in a Scottish Castle, with me as a Warrior Queen.
S   That sounds more feisty, any good?
K   Terrible. The writer-director wants to play the lead opposite

S   me.
S   Eugh!
K   There's a nice one though, set in World War Two, it's a love story again but it has got a neat twist. It would only take a couple of weeks to do. It's super low budget but I don't mind that.
S   You saying 'yes' would get them the money.
K   Obviously I know that, so do the production company. The director's an amazing woman, Cindy, do you know her, she's A.D. on the second unit here?
S   No, we never meet the second unit.
K   No, we've only crossed paths a couple of times but I think she's really got something special and she was so nice about giving me the script.
S   There is absolutely no way on this earth that Angela will let you make that film.
K   It's my career, she's got listen to me.
S   Well, good luck with that one.
K   Oh I don't know; you're right, she's right; it would be such a stupid thing to do.

Terry #2
S   Terry's not your boyfriend is he?
K   No.
S   Why do you play that game?
K   It's a simple answer.
S   You don't want people to know you're single.
K   I don't want them to know I'm gay.
S   Dear, aren't we beyond that now?
K   How many roles are there for gay women in films, mainstream films?
S   I think as an actor you're allowed to pretend to be someone you're not.
K   To an extent. Real life pollutes the fiction.
     [Wig on]
     [LX 32: Switch]
     [LX 32.5: Switch]

Sue's Mum
S   I did my best.
K/Mo It's not over, there's still time.
S   It was so difficult, she was so unreasonable, it was so tough

with Tony.
K/Mo You did your best. We all do our best.
S I'm not sure we do. I think some of us just do what's best for ourselves.
K/Mo Not you.
S I shouldn't have taken on so much. I should have given her more time.
K/Mo She was who she was; different kids react in different ways to the same thing.
S It was just so difficult.
K/Mo I know.
S She was so demanding and then she stopped demanding anything and I stopped seeing her and even you couldn't get anything out of her and you were the only one she would talk to.
K/Mo Sometimes it's too intense between mother and daughter, isn't it?
S Sometimes. Yes, sometimes it is.
What did you talk about?
K/Mo All sorts: her life mostly, you and Tony, her ambitions, you when you were young, what we could see from my window, the leaves changing colour.
S What did you say about me?
K/Mo How you had opportunities I didn't have and how proud I was of you for taking them.
S Really? You didn't say that to me at the time.
K/Mo So I'm saying it to you now.
S Now it's too late.
K/Mo She did what she did but it's not too late.
S We never talked like that.
K/Mo Sometimes it's easier to talk to your grandmother.
S Maybe, but you'd hope your daughter would at least like you.
K/Mo You do don't you? She does.
S Why would she? I didn't prioritise her. She just got the frayed left over husk of me. I traded her growing up for what?
K/Mo A scrapbook, some memories, a failed marriage, a flat you never spend time in, a credit that scrolls by as people are walking to the exit.
S Yes and you were there for us all the time.
K/Mo And I loved that and then sometimes I got so frustrated I had to lock myself away from you all, bury my head in the pillows and scream.

S   I didn't realise.
K/Mo Good. Don't you ever feel like that?
S   No.
K/Mo Good. I'm glad. She's waiting for you to call her.
S   I don't have her number.
K/Mo Maybe I did, somewhere, in those papers.
   [Wipes to Emily]
   [LX 33: Video moment and green screen]

This Year's Most Beautiful
K/Gr "Sweetie, I know all this seems so important to you now. It feels so desperate and strange I know but trust me, you will be fine, because we are always fine. Have I ever told you the story of when I was your age and ran away from home?"
   [LX 34: Awards]
   [Emily takes wig and make up off]

Sue's Speech
S   Thank you, thank you this is amazing, thank you.

   Oh, there are so many people I need to thank. I'd like to thank Pablo and Mike and everyone on *This Year's Most Beautiful*, and of course I've got to thank my team Tina, Bev, Andy and Jo it wouldn't have been possible without you, thank you.

Wow, this is amazing, it's been a long journey and I genuinely never thought I'd get here. I've never even been nominated for anything before so to win this is quite unbelievable.

Of course we don't do it for these, it's a tough job and we do it because we love it and I have loved every minute of it. Thank you.

I'm sorry. I know I'm running out of time but I need to say this. They're hands not wands. Lexi, my love, if you're watching. I miss you. Please call me. Thank You
[LX 35: Full return]

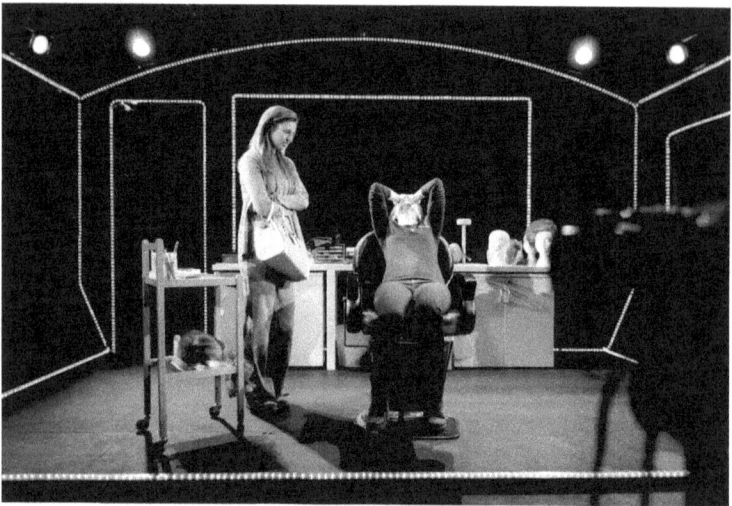

Wrap Party
K   *[Standing ready to leave]* So that's it then.
S   Yes. That's it.
K   It's a wrap.
S   It's a wrap.
K   Thank you Sue, thank you so much, you've been brilliant. I've got you a present. It's only small.
S   Oh Kate thank you, you are so sweet. There was no need, you've helped me. I'll treasure this. Thank you.
K   You are coming to the wrap party aren't you?
S   No.

K   Oh please come, you must.
S   I've got to pack up here. I've got an early start tomorrow for my Dad and there's a bottle of wine I've been saving at the B&B.
K   Oh don't be so boring! Come and have a dance, it'll be great, we'll have fun, everyone's coming.
S   Next time. At the premiere, I promise.
K   That'll be ages.
S   I'll look forward to it.
K   *[Excited]* Will you do my make up for that and the publicity tour?
S   The media junket? No, that's not really my thing.
K   Oh. What about the next film, you will be on that won't you? That's your thing. You said you would. I'll insist. You'll be there for me won't you?
S   To turn you into Tarzan?
K   Or take me back to World War 2.
S   I'd love to.
K   Honestly, I've realised, I can't do this without you, I need you.
S   You can and you will. I'm not special, there are lots of people can do what I do.
K   That's not true.
S   This time it happened to be me, next time, if it's someone else, they'll do a great job, maybe better than me, but it won't matter, you've matured so much just on this shoot. You're growing stronger. You can do anything you choose now, whatever you set your mind to. You're good you are. You don't need me, won't need me, but if you do *[hands her a card]*.
K   Thank you. Thank you. Sue.
S   Go.
K   Bye.
     [LX 36: Close w/Kate exit]

The Anderson Shelter *[pre-recorded audio and video].*

K   Stephanie Anderson… I love you.
     [LX 37: w/Sue exit]
     [LX 38: FBO]
     [LX 39: Calls]
     [LX 40: Post set]

Original Production Credits

Devised & Performed by Alexis Tuttle & Emily Holyoake
Devising & Make Up Design: Andrew Whiteoak
Direction & Script: James Yarker
Music & Sound: Nina West
Soundtrack Text: Craig Stephens
Soundtrack Voices:
Craig Stephens – Jessica Coller – Ella Speirs – Wayne Matley
Design: Harry Trow
Video: Oliver Clark
Lighting: Simon Bond
Costume: Kay Wilton
Technician: Laura Sprake
Photography: Graeme Braidwood
Set Construction: Ebrahim Nazier & Margaret Rees
Production Assistant (Stan's Cafe): Marlien van Liempt
Production Manager (The REP): Laura Killeen
Administration: Rowena Wilding & Jessica Coller
Executive Producer: Roisin Caffrey
Presented with Birmingham Repertory Theatre

With thanks to
Saima Razzaq – Cathryn Brown – Claire Woollard – Nicholas Arnold
Gaynor Arnold – Jo Gleave – Kelly Forbes – Hannah Forbes
David Edmunds – Annabel Turpin – Louise Wilkin and all at REACH
Amy McCoy – Lara Ratnaraja – Kaye Winwood – Eve Yarker
Phil Hayes – Viv Hew.
Wigs Up North & UKMUA
Laura Hargreaves & Neill Gorton at Neill's Materials
Alice Lennon & all at PAM London.
Katie Wrigley & all the ladies at UKMUA & Wigs up North
Tattooednow

Very special thanks to
Mark Coulier, Colum Mangan and Jocelyn Bennet Snewin
at Coulier Creatures FX

Original Programme Note

Made Up was inspired by the challenge of creating a show with a make up artist. This led us to the North East of England to talk to groups of (mostly) women about their relationship with make up. Their thoughts and experiences are woven into the script.

Usually in a theatre show, as in life, make up helps define a character's identity, in *Made Up* we play with this idea and twist it a little. You will find the actors changing character without changing appearance while make up is applied to change characters more slowly. This allows us to tell the story of two women sharing time together in a safe private space.

Made Up has been great fun and a great challenge to make. Alexis has had to learn how to apply make up whilst acting and Emily has had to learn to act whilst often remaining totally still. This is a gentle show, with threads of story to pick up and drop and hopefully some thoughts and feelings which will resonate with all our lives.

We hope you enjoy it and we hope to see you again.

This is our 25 Anniversary Year there is much more fun to come, please don't miss out: sign up, like, follow, bring your friends.

The Making Of Made Up

When it was decided that my wife's niece would enrol on a professional make up course talk turned to whether, as a theatre director, I could get her some work experience. In explaining that not only had Stan's Cafe never employed a make up artist but neither had any company I knew, I started to ask myself why not and if we did then what show might provoke that need.

Obviously if you were to employ a make up artist you'd want to get your money's worth from them, basically you'd want them on the stage in the show. A make up artist on stage should probably play a make up artist and this led to thoughts about the close relationship that can build up between a hair-dresser and their client; about relationships between role playing, make up and daily life, also about the various meanings of the term 'made up'.

The idea of putting an actual make up artist on stage was quickly shelved as too restricting on the show's dramatic range, instead we decided to recruit someone to design all the 'looks' and then teach an actor how to apply them.

Andrew Whiteoak was a perfect collaborator, after years of experience in theatre he had moved into film and television and so came to us with a theatrical sensibility and stories from the world our play was to be set in. Our opening challenge to Andrew was to identify the most spectacular and contrasting make up looks he could imagine moving between in 70 minutes of stage time.

These looks and the most practical sequence for them, gave us a series of landmarks to build a narrative around, some became located within the actor's professional life via moments of video using green screen technology, while others were located within the make up artist's personal life.

All this material was then written and worked up in discussion with actors Alexis Tuttle and Emily Holyoake and production assistant Marlien van Liempt. We fed in thoughts and anecdotes from research conducted with women's groups in the North East of England and ended up with the script you have in your hand now.

Framed

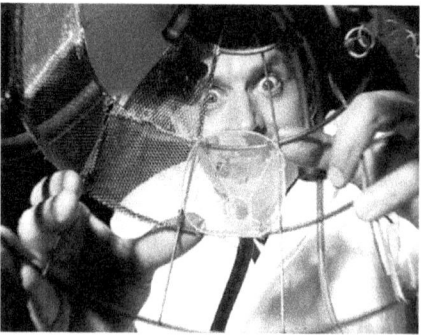

Framed was commissioned by Croydon Clocktower who wanted a performance for its public spaces to engage the public. *Framed* reimagines the building as a series of film sets and deploys its visitors as extras, body doubles and make up artists. For a two week period Stan's Cafe became film crew shooting in various locations around the building and producing a 15 minute, black and white, silent film.

Framed is a film with live action, that tells the story of Dr. Krank who makes an incredible rejuvenating face cream by draining the youth from small children. Following a child's death Krank resolves to stop manufacturing his cream. He meets Lavinia, his most powerful client, in a cafe, to tell her the news. She is furious and storms out causing Betty, the waitress, to spill tea over Krank. Betty and Krank fall in love and she persuades him to destroy his equipment and start a new life with her. Lavinia, however, has other ideas, she steals Krank's equipment and has him shot. He survives but is sent to prison. Betty helps Krank escape before breaking into Lavinia's house, setting fire to his equipment and retrieving his precious formula book. The film ends with Lavinia perishing as flames engulf her house and Krank destroying his formula so that he and Betty can happily grow old together.

Framed premiered at the end of an evening of short films, as part of Croydon Film Festival. Swift editing allowed shots of audience and actors arriving in a stretch limousine at the start of the event to be included in the film. Eventually the film's narrative includes its own screening at which point live action in venue is duplicated on the screen. Ultimately the film stops and its audience ushered outside to witness the final scene being shot as the Clocktower appears to be on fire.

Framed: Screen Play

The video is presented in black and white, it is acted and edited following stylistic devices inspired by silent movies. Cards replace dialogue, music replaces sound effects.

Scene 1: Mansion House Living Room (Private shoot)

A stately home, black gloved hands put a champagne bottle and glass on a salver. The salver is carried up grand stairs and through smart corridors. In a smart drawing room Happy 100th Birthday cards line a mantelpiece. The champagne is opened. Cucumber slices are taken off Bernadette's eyes.

Servant: Happy Birthday M'am.
Bernadette: Cheers.

She knocks the champagne back in one and reaches for a pot of face cream. It has run out. She is horrified.

Bernadette: Get me Doctor Krank!

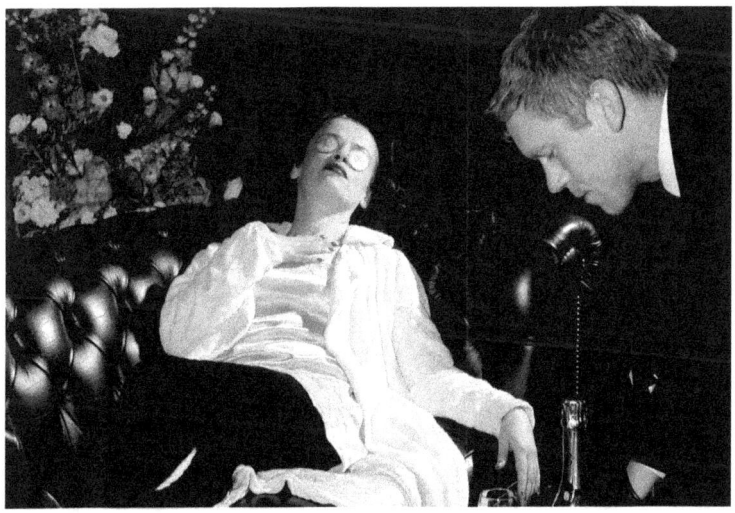

Scene 2: Scientist's Laboratory (Set piece)

Young kids wearing a helmet covered in wires and tubes wriggle around under electric shocks. They become older, looking strangely like their parents, they have had the youth sucked out of them.

Graeme, mad scientist, collects youth serum with this strange apparatus and makes it into face cream. He checks figures and formula in his little black book.

Graeme is tending one of his 'patients'. When they die in the chair he panics.

Scene 3: Cafe Opera (Set piece)

A waitress works behind the counter. Graeme is waiting in a cafe looking haggard. Bernadette arrives and strides through the chairs.

Bernadette:	*[Toward the counter]* Girl! A tea, with plenty of lemon. Doctor Krank, how lovely to see you. Please sit down.
Graeme:	Lavinia I'm sorry but...
Bernadette:	M'am, to you Doctor Krank.
Graeme:	M'am, I'm sorry but I have no more cream for you. I have decided, there will be no more cream.
Bernadette:	You have 'decided'?
Graeme:	Yes, someone died, we can't continue like this.
Bernadette :	You have 'decided', who are you to 'decide'?
Graeme:	It's my formula.
Bernadette:	It's my inspiration.
Graeme:	It's my work.
Bernadette:	It was my money.
Graeme:	It's my invention.
Bernadette:	Yes and now it is invented your job is done, I don't need you any more.
Graeme:	You do, you need my equipment, only I know how to use it.
Bernadette:	This is your final chance, will you make me more cream?
Graeme:	No, and you can't make me.
Bernadette:	I won't need to Charles.

Furious, Bernadette storms off, knocking into Heather who spills tea over Graeme.

Graeme:	Aaaah.
Heather:	I'm sorry, I'm sorry.
Graeme:	Can't you watch what you're doing!

Scene 4: Art Gallery (Small public shoot)

Heather is looking at delicate cups and saucers in an exhibition, when Graeme arrives.

Graeme:	Hello. Listen, I'm sorry about yesterday.
Heather:	So am I

Graeme:	I know it wasn't your fault.
Heather:	Your friend knocked into me.
Graeme:	I know, listen, would you let me buy you a drink, to apologise?
Heather:	Thank you, that would be lovely.

Scene 5: Bar (Small public shoot)

A montage of Heather and Graeme, laughing and drinking together, falling in love.

Scene 6: Boiler Room (Private shoot)

Black gloved hands remove Graeme's lab equipment.

Scene 7: Underground Corridor (Private shoot)

Graeme is walking, unsuspecting, back to his lab. He enters the lab, sees his stuff has gone and runs back along the corridors.

Scene 8: Main Concourse (Set piece)

An idyllic street scene, snow is drifting down from the sky. Heather stands watching kids and parents going past in hats and scarves carrying Christmas presents and Christmas trees. Graeme arrives with a large bunch of flowers. Heather is excited. At first he looks around, appearing not to recognise her. His face breaks out in a smile and just when Heather thinks he is approaching with the flowers she is knocked to the ground by Bernadette, who Graeme embraces.

Scene 9: Main Concourse (Set piece)

Heather snaps out of her daydream distressed. She looks at her watch. To her right she sees Graeme stagger, his stomach covered in blood, to a bannister railing. He topples over the railing and falls to the bottom of the stairs. He crawls from the stairs towards Heather, she starts towards him. He is grabbed by a pair of black gloved hands. They take a black formula book from his pocket. A moment later another set of hands appear to grab Graeme and drag him off. Heather looks on stunned.

Scene 10: Library (Small public shoot)

Graeme is logged into a modern maximum security prison where he wanders the corridors. He writes Heather a long letter. Later he receives a letter back, it is apparently full of junk but Graeme smiles, looks furtively round and starts wiring things together. He escapes using a strange device with LEDs on it.

Scene 11: Town Hall (Private shoot)

Bernadette is putting on make up, dressing up for a party.

Scene 12: Library Roof (Private shoot)

Graeme sneaks off, up and over the roof.

Scene 13: Outside & Inside Braithwaite Hall (Documentary)

Stretch limousines pull up. Guests get out. Bernadette greets guests. Guests help themselves to drinks and are seated at large banquet tables. This scene is shot at the start of Saturday's event and edited into the film whilst the event takes place.

Scene 14: Around Town Hall Building (Private shoot)

Heather sneaks into the Town Hall, creeps around corridors, finds Graeme's lab equipment and sets fire to it. She creeps along further corridors and cautiously opens a door.

Scene 15: Braithwaite Hall (Live)

A door edges open in the film and live onto the Braithwaite Hall balcony. Heather sneaks along the balcony. Stretches out her hand and grabs Graeme's formula book. Bernadette stands up in the hall and shouts to her security guards.

Bernadette: She's after the formula, stop her!

Bernadette and the security guards chase Heather out of the exit both live and on the film.

Scene 16: Town Hall Steps (Set Piece)

[Pre-recorded] Heather is chased out of the burning mansion and down the main steps by the servants. Graeme is there waiting for her. Together they beat off the servants and set fire to the formula book.

Heather: Where's Lavinia?
Graeme: I think she may have gone to rescue my equipment.

They both look up at the clocktower.

Scene 17: Braithwaite Hall - interior and exterior (Live)

The video projection stops and house lights come on.

Steward: Ladies and Gentlemen I must ask you please to gather your personal belongings together and, using the entrances at the back and front of the hall, please leave the building as calmly and safely as possible. Please gather outside on the pavement, please do not return for loved ones. I must ask you to leave the building immediately. Thank you.

Outside smoke is seen billowing out of the Clocktower and the windows are lit by flames. Bernadette is on a balcony shouting against Krank and her situation. She staggers back into the room.

"The End" is projected on the outside of the building.

Amanda: Cut! Great that's a wrap, where's the party?

End Credits

Dr. Krank: Graeme Rose
Lavinia: Bernadette Russell
Betty: Heather Burton
Muscle: Dan Skinner

Director: Amanda Hadingue

Camera Operator: James Yarker
Lighting: Craig Stephens
Sound: Sarah Archdeacon

Director: James Yarker

Editor: Joseph Potts
Music: Giles Perrin
Props: Lottie Leedham

Early sketch

We're after four major set piece scenes for public engagement. One for each of the shooting days 26, 27, 28, 29 November.

Modes of public engagement could include:
    People holding and shuffling cue cards
    People holding up / moving scenery
    People acting as extras delivering things
    Body doubles for recalcitrant stars.
    Stunt people for over precious stars
    Voice coaching for accents
    Script advisors
    Make up assistance
    Body parts in shot
    Acting as wind machines off screen
    Clapper board person
    Donate props to the cause
    Sound effects

The way I'm thinking of the casting at the moment is some permutation of:
    Actor 1 Amanda / Heather / Sarah
    Actor 2 Graeme
    Director Nick / Craig / Amanda
    Camera operator = James
    Sound operator = Sarah / Craig
    Stage manager / props = Craig / Heather

Essentially these are all roles in the 'theatre' of making the film. As camera operator I don't expect to engage with anything other than shooting the footage we're after for the final video. Everyone else will have more of an eye on the 'theatre' than the 'video' during public shoots.

There is also the opportunity for a series of guest stars to appear, one per day possibly?

Guest Stars: Nominations please...

The film could be quite expressionistic, but the scenes we are shooting live should probably be fairly conventional at heart. Narratively there is obvious fun to be had if the two actors are playing lovers on screen and hate each other off screen.

Locations

The Clocktower complex offers a host of locations, some fully open to the public, some occasionally open to the public, the others private. In brief they are:
- A big busy bright cafe
- A small red brick bar
- A glass fronted library
- An internal courtyard (modern)
- The building's grand exterior
- A museum including mock up of old dentist's surgery
- An art gallery which will be housing an exhibition of sculpture
- A cinema
- A grand hall with balcony and faux book cases
- The council chamber (which acts as the court room on *The Bill*)
- Council rooms and main double staircase (very grand)
- An old box office booth
- An old style boiler room and its control room
- Underground corridors with pipes along the ceiling
- A huge wall safe
- A bridge between buildings with windows on both sides and views of office blocks

There is a video club at the Clocktower who can act as a second unit for us, shooting footage to a brief we give them.

The final, fifth performance day, Saturday 30th November, is the day of the video premiere. We will compere an evening of kids video screenings for the Croydon Film Festival with their attendant awards ceremony. Then our video will be screened (I imagine this lasting 15 minutes tops). I imagine the video's narrative either being open-ended with the conclusion provided live on the night at the premiere or the live intervention interrupting the video which then continues to a conclusion after the intervention. For example, the video may lead to a romantic meal between the two main protagonists. We cut to live video relay of the two actors at their table at the awards ceremony having a big row, one chasing the other out of the room and the video picking up again following their chase but pre-recorded.

I'm trying to persuade Rick to do the soundtrack.

That's it so far. Pitch...

Further ideas on Framed project

REVISED PERFORMANCE DATE
The festival want to programme the premiere on the Saturday 30th Nov now NOT Sunday 1st Dec.

A large portion of the project feels like it will be spent in preparation. This should happen steadily between now and then as the time we are all available together to work on it is limited, possibly, to the week of 18th November.

In view of this, could we arrange any Mondays together in September / October depending on people's availability (knowing Amanda has some Monday's off from The Unicorn at some point)?

Each day's big 'set piece' public interaction scene may last approximately 20 minutes?

We should look to establish attitudes between the various crew members and cast to be played through the filming.

It is suggested that the video itself is made in an expressionistic style. This will differentiate it sharply from the atmosphere of the filming that led to it. It will contrast the production with the many other video projects already made around the building. It could make a fun point of tension if the actors think they are in a more conventional film whilst camera operator and director are conspiring to shoot some Art House masterpiece.

The expressionism may extend to dumping all the video's live text in the editing and dubbing in a fake foreign language. As well as providing a strange dark / hilarious edge to the video this device could liberate us from having to record high quality convincing sound live on set with the distractions of the public around the shoot.

If the premiere is set out a bit like the BAFTAs with white tablecloths on round tables we could make the video's live finale some strange business about someone standing up 'through' the table in some 'ghostly' way which is strange enough to frighten off the unwitting leads but is ultimately daft and a triumph for the director and camera operator.

One of the 'guest stars' for the production could be Mark Anderson who we could collaborate with in the 'burning down' of the Clocktower.

A smallish scale scene could be the filming of people casually walking into the Clocktower with the director / stage manager shouting urging people not to look at the camera.

James 2/9/2

More Framed thoughts

Hello folks

I've been doing a bit of serious thinking over the last couple of days and have come up with this 'treatment'. I realised it would be much easier if, rather than guest stars, we just had a third character. This character has been called Ursula after Martinez, because she was in my mind as I wrote it but I'm not committed to that and haven't asked her. There are a fair number of low level props required but we can get someone in to acquire those for us. Don't be alarmed, I know it looks ambitious but careful reading will show it's not so bad.

There are four set piece scenes:
    A 'death' scene as discussed.
    A 'cafe' scene as discussed.
    An escape come crowd, come fight scene (Heather has been
    booked to work with a drama group for two sessions before
    we arrive. She can rehearse them up for this scene).
    Perhaps most controversially, a trial scene.

There are four smaller public scenes, which we can be much more functional about filming. This draws from Amanda's notion of getting the public to play very small roles and shooting rapidly:
    Library
    Dentist's Chair in museum
    Art Gallery
    Bar

There are then four scenes to be shot in private. Which we can be very functional about, so they won't take long:
    Roof

      Town Hall with Ursula
      Town Hall with Heather
      Boiler Room

There is a location montage of Rio De Janeiro (Craig's top idea)*.

There is the element of shooting people's arrivals at the premiere and editing it into the film as I had originally hoped.

There is also the live action moment.

You will notice that the rooftop fire has been moved to the Saturday premiere event so it plays more usefully with the live / recorded narrative edge.

Tell me what you think. There is much work to do but I've relaxed a bit and feel more confident with something in place to at least discuss. I've pretty much recruited an editor. I'm still holding out for Rick on the soundtrack.

Lisa at the Clocktower wrote yesterday saying should she have an image and copy by the end of the week. I doubt anyone will be able to read this image but I've attached it just in case. The copy is here as well. All comments welcome.

---

* Stan's Cafe was due to be performing in Rio immediately before going to Croydon for *Framed*.

About the illustration and design

The illustrations for the covers of these books were undertaken by students at Birmingham City University as the final module of their first-year illustration course during the Spring/Summer of 2018. The images were developed through workshops using variations of the theatre-devising methods employed by Stan's Cafe but adapted and applied to the making of visual work. The resulting work was shown in the pop-up exhibition *The Something Of Somebody Something* at Stan's Cafe's venue @AE Harris in May 2018.

The design concept of the books was produced by final year Graphic Design student Aimee Chapman. These were then further developed for print in a collaborative process between Stan's Cafe and the University's Innovation Product Support Service (IPSS) which involved helping the company to select appropriate DTP software, undertaking training and selecting a suitable print on demand service.

Gareth Courage
Lecturer in Illustration
Birmingham City University

www.ingramcontent.com/pod-product-compliance
Lightning Source LLC
Chambersburg PA
CBHW071757080526
44588CB00013B/2276